Strange ... But True?

ELIZABETH NOLL

BLACK
RABBIT
BOOKS

Bolt is published by Black Rabbit Books
P.O. Box 3263, Mankato, Minnesota, 56002.
www.blackrabbitbooks.com
Copyright © 2017 Black Rabbit Books

Design and Production by Michael Sellner
Photo Research by Rhonda Milbrett

Library of Congress Control Number: 2015954847

HC ISBN: 978-1-68072-022-8   PB ISBN: 978-1-68072-292-5

Printed in the United States at CG Book Printers,
North Mankato, Minnesota, 56003. PO #1795 4/16

Image Credits
AP Images: 16; Corbis:
Kathleen Finlay, 15; Dreamstime:
Rolffimages, 1, 14–15; iStock: Achim
Prill, 10; agsandrew, 3, 6; FotografiaBasica,
9; Highwaystarz-Photography, 22; Yuri_Arcurs,
13; Shutterstock: agsandrew, Cover (face), 21,
32; Alex Mit, Cover (brain), Back Cover, 31; An-
drey_Kuzmin, 20; Bruce Rolff, 27 (top); CLIPAREA
l Custom media, 18–19; Fer Gregory, 27 (bottom);
koya979, 28; Leremy, 24–25; SkillUp, 12–13;
Vasilyev Alexandr, 4–5
Every effort has been made to contact copyright holders for material reproduced
in this book. Any omissions will be
rectified in subsequent printings
if notice is given to the
publisher.

Contents

CHAPTER 1

Was It a

In the dark of night, a man shot awake. He had dreamed his son was very sick. The dream felt so real, he called the doctor. The boy was close to death.

HOW MANY
AMERICANS
BELIEVE IN
PARANORMAL
ACTIVITIES

41%
ESP

37%
HAUNTED
HOUSES

ESP

Some people say the father's dream was an extra **sense** called **ESP**. Believers think there are many kinds of ESP. One kind allows someone to read minds. Another kind lets a person see events happening far away. A third kind lets a person know the future.

Many people believe in ESP. But many others do not. They say **psychics** pretend to have special powers.

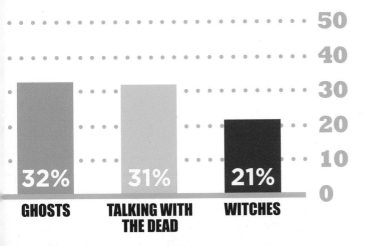

32%	31%	21%
GHOSTS	TALKING WITH THE DEAD	WITCHES

CHAPTER 2

What Is

Many people think they have ESP. They say they know who is going to call before the phone rings. Others say they dreamed about something before it happened.

Another kind of ESP might be the ability to talk to the dead.

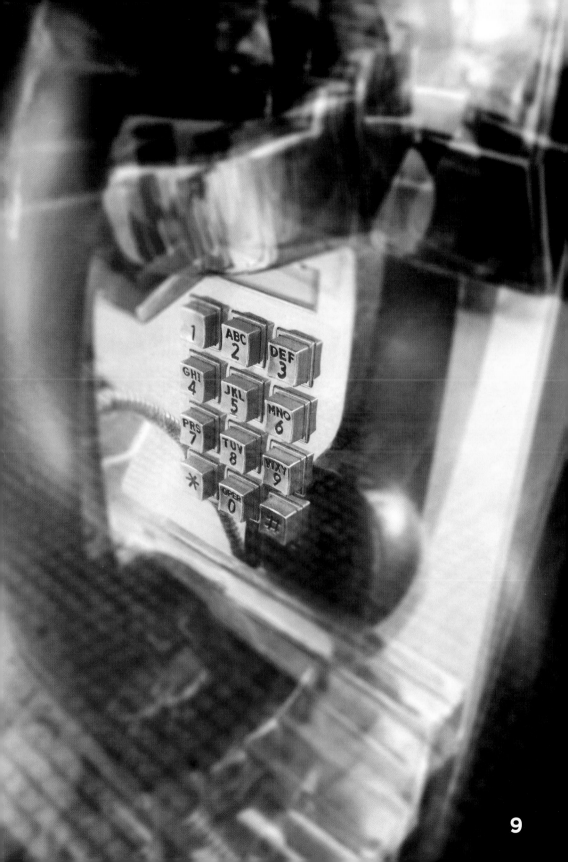

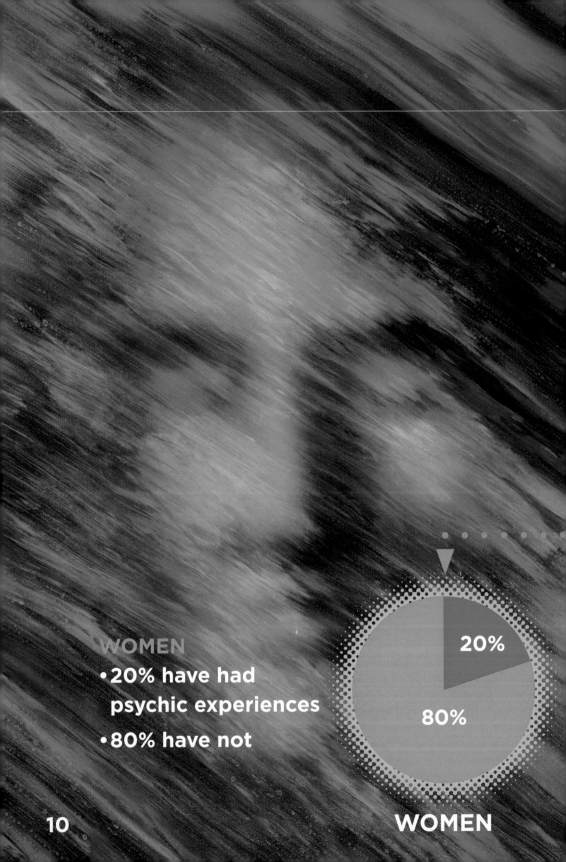

WOMEN
- 20% have had
  psychic experiences
- 80% have not

20%

80%

WOMEN

Bad Feeling

Some people claim to know when something bad is about to happen. The warnings might come as bad dreams. Other times, it's just a feeling that something is wrong.

Comparing Experiences in Men and Women

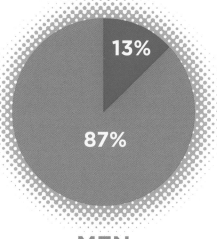

13%

87%

MEN
- 13% have had psychic experiences
- 87% have not

MEN

Using ESP

People who claim to have ESP have worked on police cases. They have tried to find missing people. Believers think ESP helped solve some cases.

CROSS • CRIME SCENE DO NOT CROSS

CRIME SCENE DO NOT CROSS • CRIM

People in ancient Greece believed a fortune-teller **predicted** the future. Did this fortune-teller have ESP? Nobody knows.

CHAPTER 3

Events

Believers say stories about ESP prove it's real. In one story, a mother dreamed the light over her baby's crib fell. She woke up and took the baby out of bed. About two hours later, the light fell, smashing the crib.

15

Train Wreck

In another story, a boy asked if his aunt and uncle had been in a train **wreck**. His father said no. But the boy said he had seen the accident. The next day, they found out their family had been in a train wreck.

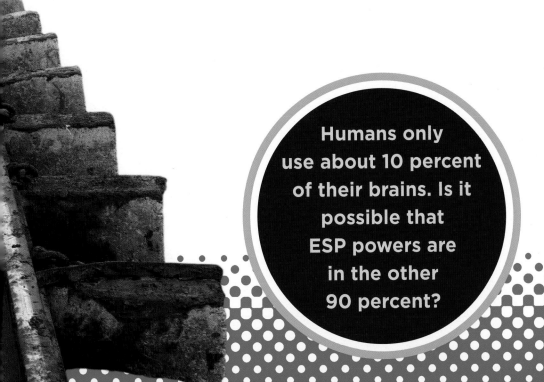

Humans only use about 10 percent of their brains. Is it possible that ESP powers are in the other 90 percent?

STRANGE FEELINGS

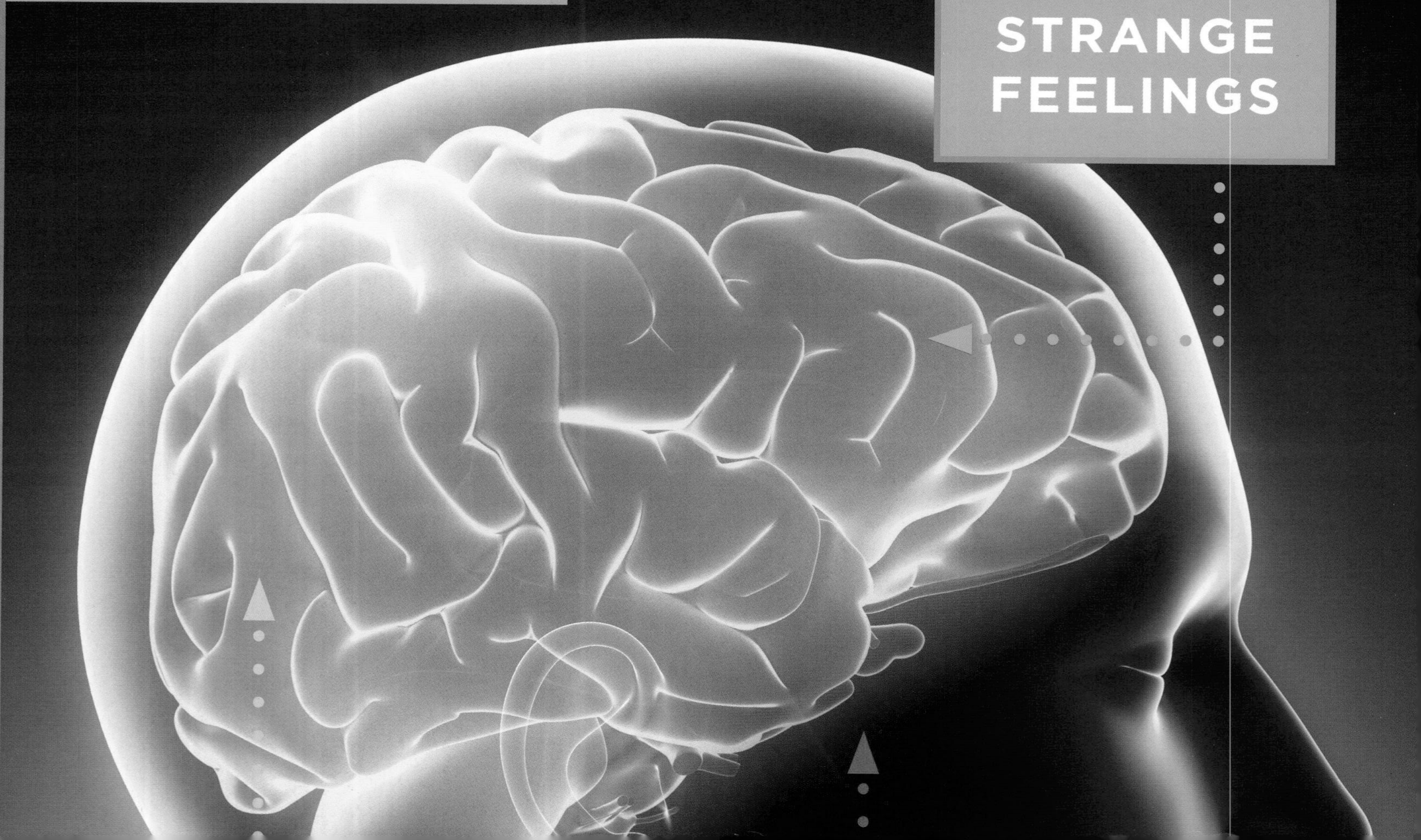

USING 10%
BRAIN POWER

LITTLE SCIENTIFIC PROOF

PERSONAL
STORIES

Long Distance

Some stories talk about people hearing others' thoughts. One person claims to hear what his brother is thinking. His brother lives 3,000 miles (4,828 kilometers) away!

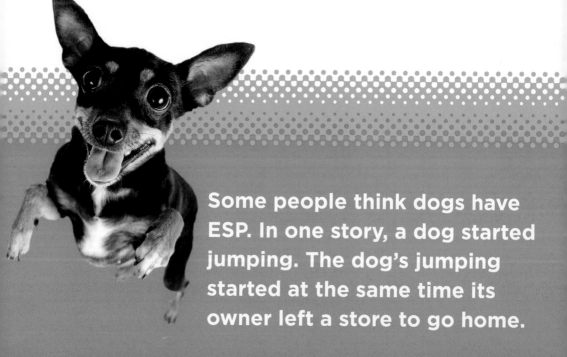

Some people think dogs have ESP. In one story, a dog started jumping. The dog's jumping started at the same time its owner left a store to go home.

21

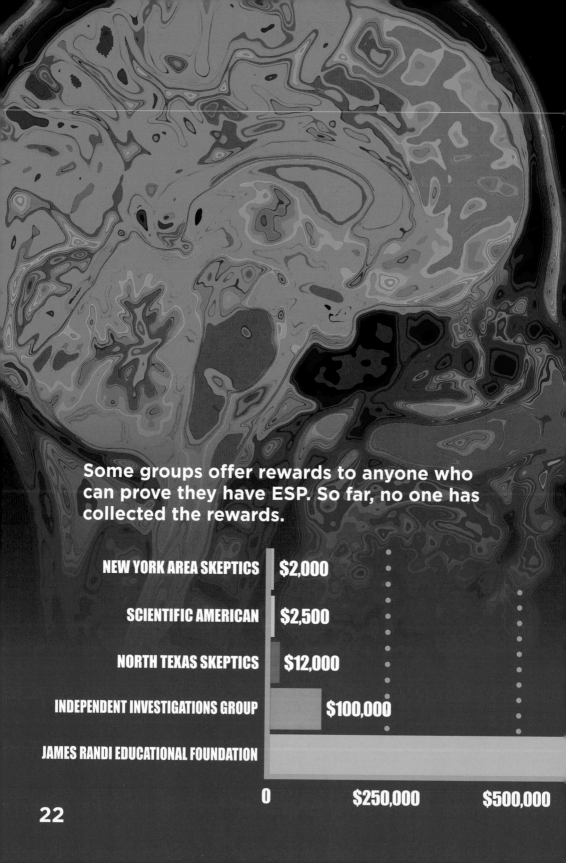

Some groups offer rewards to anyone who can prove they have ESP. So far, no one has collected the rewards.

NEW YORK AREA SKEPTICS	$2,000
SCIENTIFIC AMERICAN	$2,500
NORTH TEXAS SKEPTICS	$12,000
INDEPENDENT INVESTIGATIONS GROUP	$100,000
JAMES RANDI EDUCATIONAL FOUNDATION	

0          $250,000 $500,000

CHAPTER 4

Searching for Answers

Many people believe ESP stories are made up. Scientists have tested people who say they have ESP. No one has passed the tests.

Scientists have also used brain scans to find out about ESP. They think ESP would show up in brain activity. But they haven't found any **evidence** of ESP.

$1,000,000

$750,000 $1,000,000

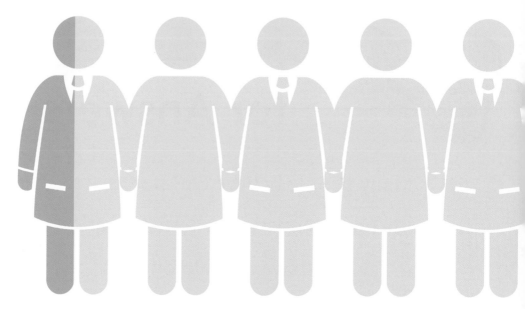

Only about 4 in 100 scientists believe in ESP.

About 41 out of 100 people in the general population believe.

 = 10 people

What Do You Think?

It is true that some people pretend to have ESP. And scientists have not proven that ESP is real. But could events, such as the mother saving her baby, be proof? What do you think?

Zener Cards

• •

Past scientists used Zener cards to test for ESP. They asked people to guess which shape they would show next. The average person got one out of five right.

Believe It or Not?

Answer the questions below.
Then add up your points to
see if you believe.

1 **You have a dream about your friend getting hurt. What do you do?**

A. Go to him or her now! (3 points)

B. Send a quick text to make sure
   he or she is OK. (2 points)

C. Go back to sleep. (1 point)

2 Are parts of the brain working in ways we can't explain?

A. Definitely! (3 points)

B. Maybe. (2 points)

C. No. Scientists would see that on scans. (1 point)

3 You suddenly have a bad feeling as you walk into a room. What do you think?

A. Something terrible is going to happen. I know it. (3 points)

B. Weird. I wonder why I felt like that. (2 points)

C. Must have eaten something bad for lunch. (1 point)

. . . .

3 points:
There's no way you think ESP is real.

4–8 points:
Maybe it's real. But then again, maybe it's not.

9 points:
You're a total believer!

29

ability (uh-BIL-uh-tee)—the power or skill to do something

ESP—stands for extrasensory perception

evidence (EH-vuh-dens)—something that shows something else exists or is true

predict (pre-DIKT)—to say something will happen in the future

psychic (SI-kik)—describes strange mental powers and abilities; it's also a person who claims to have unnatural mental abilities.

sense (SENS)—one of five natural powers from which you receive information; the five senses are touch, taste, smell, sight, and hearing.

wreck (REK)—an accident in which a vehicle is badly damaged

BOOKS

Green, Carl R. *Astonishing Mind Powers. Investigating the Unknown.* Berkeley Heights, NJ: Enslow Publishers, 2012.

Owings, Lisa. *ESP.* Unexplained Mysteries. Minneapolis: Bellwether Media, Inc., 2015.

Perish, Patrick. *Is ESP Real?* Unexplained: What's the Evidence? Mankato, MN: Amicus, 2014.

WEBSITES

ESP Is Put to the Test—Can You Foretell the Results?
news.nationalgeographic.comnews/2014/01/140121-esp-clairvoyance-sixth-sense-science-telepathy/

ESP: What Can Science Say?
undsci.berkeley.edu/article/esp

What Is ESP?
www.ucalgary.ca/pip369/mod10/extrasensory/esp

INDEX